PLANES

Andrew Langley

W

FRANKLIN WATTS
LONDON•SYDNEY

An Appleseed Editions book

First published in 2010 by Franklin Watts
338 Euston Road, London NW1 3BH

Franklin Watts Australia
Hachette Children's Books
Level 17/207 Kent St, Sydney, NSW 2000

© 2010 Appleseed Editions

Created by Appleseed Editions Ltd,
Well House, Friars Hill, Guestling,
East Sussex TN35 4ET

Planning and production by Discovery Books Limited
Designed by D.R. ink
Cover design by Blink Media
Edited by James Nixon

ISBN: 978 1 4451 0030 2

Dewey Classification: 629.1'3334

A CIP catalogue for this book is available from the British Library.

Photograph acknowledgements
Corbis: pp. 9 bottom (Scott T. Smith), 11 top (George Hall); Defence Images: p. 28 (© Crown Copyright/MOD,
Image from www.photos.mod.uk, Reproduced with the permission of the Controller of Her Majesty's Stationery
Office. Getty Images: pp. 7 (Annie Griffiths Belt/National Geographic), 15 (Roland Magunia/AFP), 17 (John
MacDougall/AFP), 23 top (Brent Winebrenner/Lonely Planet Images), 23 bottom (Paul Scuders), 24 (Chuck
Keeler), 25 bottom (Stringer/AFP); Library of Congress: p. 5 bottom; NASA/Dryden Flight Research Center: pp.
20 (Judson Brohmer/USAF), 21 (Tony Landis), 26, 27 bottom (Steve Lighthill), 29 top; Qinetiq: p. 29 bottom;
Shutterstock: pp. 4 (Robert Sarosiek), 5 top, 6 and 7 top (Carlos E. Santa Maria), 8 (Perry Gerenday), 9 top
(Ivan Cholakov/Gostock-dot-net), 10 top (Dejan Milinkovic), 10 bottom (Ramon Berk), 11 bottom (William Attard
McCarthy), 12, 13 (Margo Harrison), 14 (Ilja Masik), 19 top (Christopher McRae), 19 bottom (Galyna Andrushko),
22 (Randal Sedler), 25 top (Eugene Berman), 27 top; USAF: p. 18 (Staff Sgt. Cherie A. Thurlby).

Cover photos: Shutterstock: top (William Attard McCarthy), bottom (Eray Haciosmanoglu).

Printed in China

Franklin Watts is a division of Hachette Children's Books,
www.hachette.co.uk

Contents

What is a plane?

Planes can carry us high into the air and over huge distances. There are all sorts of planes, from giant passenger planes to tiny **microlights**.

Parts of a plane

Tailplane: helps to balance and steer the plane

Wings: they are shaped to create **lift**, which carries the plane into the air

Cockpit: the control centre where the pilot sits

Landing gear: wheels for landing and taking off

Fuselage: the plane's body

Engine: the motor which drives the plane along

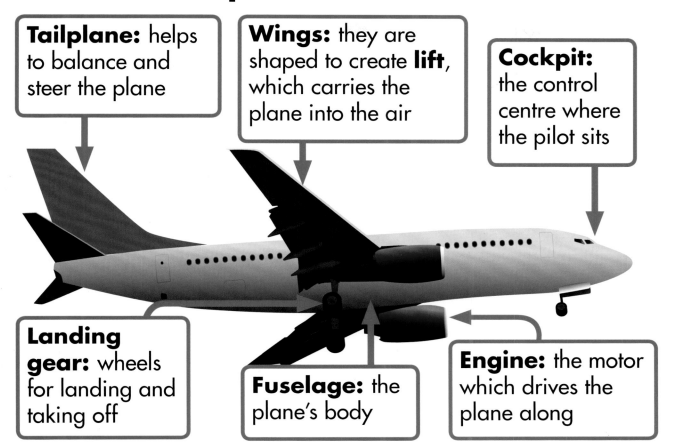

First flight

The first plane to make a proper, controlled flight was called *Flyer*. It was built in the USA in 1903 by two brothers, Orville and Wilbur Wright.

In the cockpit

The person who controls a plane is called the pilot. The pilot sits in the **cockpit**, near the front of the plane.

There are many types of controls in the cockpit.

Landing gear control: lowers the wheels

Yoke: steers the plane

Throttle: to go faster

Radar: shows if other aircraft are nearby

Controls

The **yoke** is like the steering wheel of a car. The pilot can push, pull or twist the yoke. This turns or tilts the plane.

Dials or **display screens** show important information, such as the plane's speed and height, and how much fuel is left.

Speedometer: shows speed

Altimeter: shows height

In the open

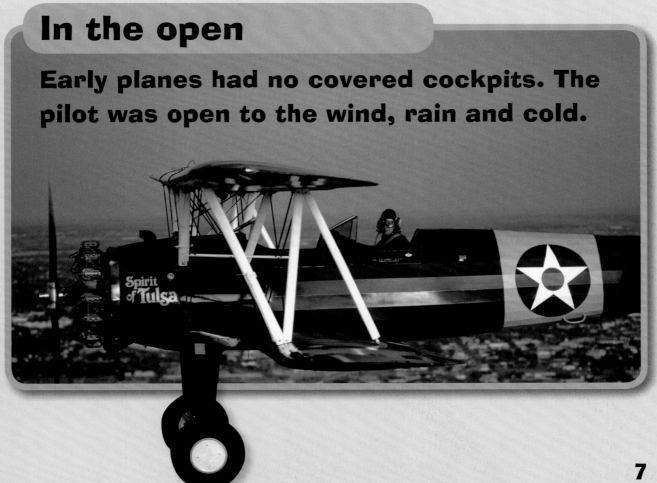

Early planes had no covered cockpits. The pilot was open to the wind, rain and cold.

Spirit of Tulsa

Propeller planes

Many planes are powered by propellers. Each propeller has its own engine. The engine turns the propeller round very fast.

Most small planes have just one propeller, set in the nose. Bigger ones have two (one on each wing) or four (two on each wing). Some planes have even more.

The propeller

A propeller is like an electric fan, with long blades sticking out. The blades are set at an angle. As they spin, they pull air in

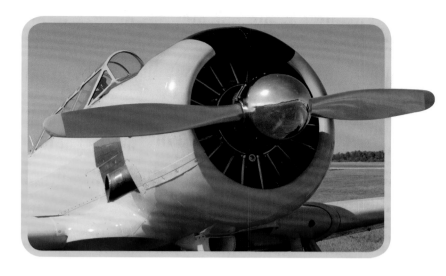

from the front and push it out behind. This drives the plane forwards.

Giant of the skies

The widest and tallest aircraft ever made had eight propellers. Called *Spruce Goose*, it was built in the USA in 1947. Its wings measured 97 metres across.

Jet planes

Planes with jet engines can travel much faster than propeller aircraft. Most fighter planes and **airliners** are powered by jets.

Jet engine

Fighter plane

Jet planes can reach very high speeds. Some can fly more than twice as fast as the **speed of sound** – over 1,300 mph (2,000 kph).

Jump jet

A 'jump jet' can take off and land vertically – like a helicopter. The nozzles of its jet engines are pointed at the ground, pushing it upwards.

Jet engine nozzle

Jet engine

Air is pulled into a jet engine at the front. It is heated by a spray of burning fuel. **Exhaust gases** shoot out of the back, driving the plane along.

Light planes

A light plane is a small and simple aircraft. It usually has a light body and a single propeller. It can take off and land on small airfields.

Tiny flyer

A microlight is the smallest and cheapest kind of plane. It is not much bigger than a car, and has very simple controls.

Light planes have hundreds of uses. They are used to train new pilots, to check overhead cables, to look for people who are lost and many other things.

Landing gear

A plane has wheels and supports for taking off and landing. This is called the landing gear. The wheels are often folded back into the wings or **fuselage** during flight.

Passenger planes

Millions of people travel by plane every year. An airliner is a big passenger plane, which can carry hundreds of travellers at a time.

Jet airliners can fly long distances at high speed. They usually fly very high, so they are above clouds and bad weather.

Autopilot

Most airliners have autopilot. This is a system that uses computers to fly the plane without a pilot.

Jumbo jet

The Airbus A380 can carry many more passengers than any other plane – over 850!

The fuselage

The fuselage is the airliner's body. It is a long tube where the crew and passengers sit. The fuselage has to be very strong.

Cargo planes

Cargo planes carry goods all over the world. Usually, this cargo goes in the fuselage.

Some planes carry small, light things that need to be delivered quickly, such as fresh flowers and fruit. Others transport huge, heavy things. This plane is carrying the Space Shuttle on its back!

Tailplane

The tailplane

The **tailplane** has an upright **fin**, which stops the rear of the plane swinging from side to side. The pilot uses hand and foot controls to move the **rudder** on the fin and change direction.

Extra room

The Airbus Beluga is one of the strangest planes you'll see. Its fuselage is very wide so that extra big loads will fit inside.

Combat planes

Combat planes are used in wartime. Their main weapons are missiles, bombs and guns.

There are two main kinds of combat plane. Fighters are fast and nimble. They attack enemy planes, or targets on the ground. Bombers are bigger. They carry heavy loads of bombs and missiles over long distances.

Missiles

Lightning strike

The F-22 Raptor is one of the fastest fighter planes ever built. It can easily fly at twice the speed of sound. Each plane costs about $137 million.

Flaps

Plane wings have movable surfaces at the back called **flaps**. The pilot uses the yoke to bend these up or down. This controls the flight of the aircraft.

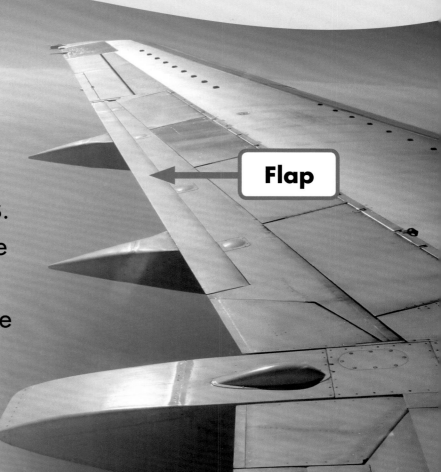

Flap

Spy planes

Some of the most important military planes carry few weapons. These are spy planes. They carry cameras and other equipment to watch the enemy on the ground.

Spy planes usually fly very high, so they are hard to spot. One of the most famous was the SR-71 Blackbird (above). This could fly at a height of 30 kilometres (18 miles) above the ground.

Radio

Pilots use special radio equipment to find their way. The radio receives signals from the ground. These show the correct course to take.

Robot plane

One of the latest spy planes has no pilot. The Global Hawk is controlled by radio from the ground.

Seaplanes

A seaplane does not need a flat airfield. It can take off and land on water.

Most seaplanes have big floats instead of wheels for their landing gear. Some even have wheels and floats. These are called **amphibians**, and can land on water or on the ground.

Float

Flying boats

Seaplanes usually have two long floats which keep the body out of the water. But a flying boat (right) has a specially shaped body, which floats in the water like a boat.

Planes on the snow

Ski planes can land on snow and even slippery ice. Instead of floats, they are fitted with skis.

Ski

Special planes

Special planes are needed for certain jobs. They are built differently from other planes.

Farmers use planes to spray chemicals on big fields of crops. The wings are fitted with nozzles that pump out the spray.

Stunt flying

Light planes are needed for aerobatics. In this sport, pilots make their planes roll, fly upside down or loop the loop.

Fighting fires

Firefighters use planes to pick up water from lakes or the sea and drop it on fires.

Modern firefighting planes have as many as four scoops fitted underneath. These can pick up 12 tonnes of water in 14 seconds.

Rocket planes

The fastest of all planes have rocket engines. They reach high speeds very quickly. But rockets burn a huge amount of fuel and are very expensive to fly.

Rocket planes can fly very high. Some have even reached the edge of space.

Rocket engine

A rocket works like a jet engine. Special chemicals are mixed inside. They burn and produce a powerful stream of exhaust gas, which pushes the rocket forwards.

Record holder

The fastest plane of all time was the NASA X-43, a pilotless rocket. In 2004, it reached a speed of 7,546 mph (12,144 kph).

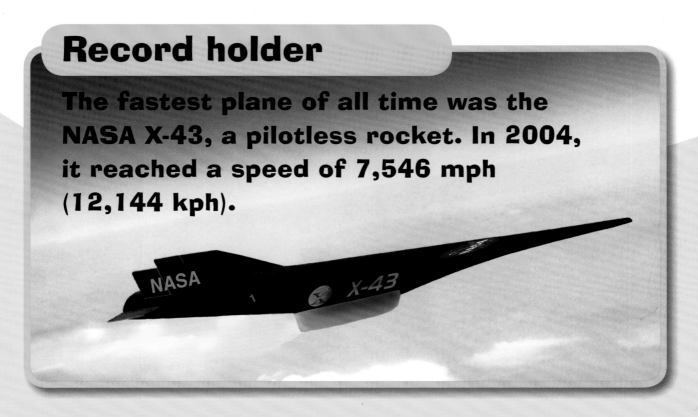

Future planes

What planes will be flying in the future? Engineers are working on many amazing new designs.

Some future planes will have new shapes. The '**flying wing**' is simply one giant wing with the cabin space inside. Other planes will use new kinds of fuel, such as **hydrogen**, instead of petrol.

The B-2 Spirit Stealth Bomber has a 'flying wing' design.

Scramjet speed

Scientists are developing an amazing plane that can fly at seven times the speed of sound. Its engine is a 'scramjet'. These engines burn hydrogen and oxygen. Scramjets have been tested on rockets (right).

Glossary

aerobatics performing stunts in a plane, such as rolls and loops

airliner a large plane, which carries passengers

altimeter instrument that shows how high a plane is flying

amphibian a plane that can take off from land or water

cockpit the place where the pilot sits to control the plane

display screen a screen which shows the speed and position of the plane. It may also show how the plane's equipment is working

exhaust gases the waste gases that are produced when fuel is burnt

fin the upright and fixed part of the tailplane

flaps movable surfaces in the wing of the plane, used to control the aircraft's flight

flying wing a plane where the cockpit and cabin space are built into one big wing

fuselage the body of a plane, where passengers or cargo are carried

hydrogen a colourless gas that is burnt for fuel

microlight a very small and light kind of plane

lift the force that makes the the plane move upwards

oxygen one of the common gases in the air we breathe

rudder the movable flap attached to the fin, used to steer a plane left or right

speed of sound the speed at which sound travels through the air (about 1,225 kph, or 760 mph)

tailplane the short wings and fin at the back of the plane

vertically straight up or down

yoke the stick used by the pilot to change a plane's direction

Index

Websites

www.sciencekidsathome.com/science_topics/flight.html
Find out how a plane takes off.

www.funpaperairplanes.com
Build your own flyers.

www.nasa.gov/audience/forstudents/K-4/stories/ames-how-planes-fly-slideshow.html
Find out how planes stay in the air.